SEVER

THE TIES

THE ROAD TO DELIVERANCE

KIMBERLY NELMS

SEVER THE TIES
The Road To Deliverance

Published by **Kimberly Nelms**

Copyright © 2022 by **Kimberly Nelms**

ISBN print: 979-8-9856100-0-0

ISBN ebook: 979-8-9856100-1-7

Disclaimer

All the information in this book is to be used only for informational and educational purposes. The author will not account for any results that stem from the use of the contents herein. While conscious and creative attempts have been made to ensure that all information provided herein is as accurate and useful as possible, the author is not legally bound to be responsible for any damage caused by the accuracy and use/misuse of this information.

Every attempt has been made to source all quotes properly.

Cover Art: JD Designs-Jordan Mitchell
Cover Design: JD Designs-Jordan Mitchell
Formatting and Interior Design: Theo H.
Printed in the United States of America
First Edition 2022

DEDICATION

This book is dedicated to everyone who has ever had to sever ties with a person, place, or thing. Just as trees shed leaves, we all have things that we'll need to remove throughout our lives. Sometimes, it could even be a thought or mindset. I want you to know that in doing this, you will ultimately become the person that you are meant to be. Thus, you will be on your way to your destiny and fulfilling your God-given purpose. Now, go and be great!

TABLE OF CONTENTS

PREFACE

This book is an inspirational and self-help book based on the personal experiences and information of the author. It discusses different things that keep us in bondage and prevent us from reaching our destiny and fulfilling our God-given purpose. Therefore, with this book, I seek to help everyone who has had to let go or is about to sever ties with unhealthy relationships or situations they've held onto for a long time by discussing the various obstacles that I faced and how I overcame them.

ACKNOWLEDGMENT

First and foremost, I want to thank God, from whom all blessings flow, for giving me the vision to write this book. He knew He could entrust me with delivering this message to His people, so, He gave it to me. Also, I thank Him for giving me strength and wisdom during my journey. I give Him all the praise and glory!

Secondly, I want to thank my husband, Marcus Nelms, for being persistent and pushing me through the process even when I got tired and almost gave up. Thank you for your continued support and love; it means the world to me. Thank you for being a sounding board.

Also, I appreciate everyone who played a part in my process of severing ties.

Special appreciations to Rich Book Authors for helping me write the vision and making it plain.

From the bottom of my heart, thank you.

INTRODUCTION

A s a little girl living in the country, there was so much I didn't know about God and Christianity. Even though I attended the Baptist church, which was my great grandfather's church and where most of my family went, it didn't make any difference.

Since I grew up with my maternal grandmother, it was only natural for us to go to church every Sunday because she always had us with her, and we couldn't go anywhere else if we didn't go to church. My cousins, sister, and I were in the youth choir, and we participated in all the other youth activities as well.

As the years rolled by, I became a member of other denominations, and I learned so much about biblical things. I began to understand how things from our past have a way of restricting us and keeping us in bondage. I learned that some of the challenges we face aren't about us. We go through those phases so we can encourage and help others get through what we've overcome.

In becoming who God ultimately wants us to be, there are certain things that we need to sever from our lives. This includes;

Family Ties – These are things that we deal with in our family and during our childhood that may have an adverse effect on our adult life.

Generational Ties–These are curses and things from our lineage that can destroy us.

Demonic Ties - These are evil spirits and strongholds that prevent us from spiritual deliverance.

Soul Ties - These can either be good or bad. They are connections that we make through our souls. While good soul ties help us to grow and walk in our God-given purpose, bad soul ties, on the other hand, destroy our purpose through distractions. Distractions can kill us and our divine purpose.

Traumatic Ties - These are those painful experiences we go through that can stunt our growth. They can also cause stress and bondage.

Transitional Ties - These are ties that hinder you from evolving spiritually beyond your current state. It can be anything the enemy uses, for example, people, things, or even emotions.

Destiny Ties - These are all the things that tie you to the purpose God has for your life. They are the things you experience that shape you spiritually and help you reach your destiny.

I will explain some of my personal experiences in this book, and I'll also provide more information about the various ties discussed above and how they affect our lives.

CHAPTER 1

FAMILY TIES

"Train up a child in the way he should go; even when he is old, he will not depart from it."-**Proverbs 22:6**

For you to be who God has called you to be, there are many things you must sever ties with. Although the process to sever these ties may be tedious, strenuous, and sometimes painful, it is necessary. Also, you must sever ties with any negative emotion or characteristics that you may possess, such as unforgiveness, anger, bitterness, jealousy, etc.

While most people don't even realize that they are wrestling with things that they need to be delivered from, others are in denial. Unfortunately, being in denial only delays and hinders the process of deliverance.

Research has shown that talking to a trusted person gives you a feeling of freedom. Therefore, there are several people who are willing and qualified to help you through your healing process. Therapists and spiritual leaders are at the top of my list of recommended people to seek counsel from. Although this may be the hardest and most painful step in seeking deliverance from unhealthy ties, it is highly recommended.

Mere talking may work for some situations, while some other situations may require more work to discover the things you need to unpack. This is because the roots are

The experiences you have and the lessons you learned during your childhood build a foundation as an adult.

deeply embedded and have existed for a long time. For example, the issues that some people have to deal with in their adulthood are the effects of things that started or happened as far back as their childhood.

Your childhood plays a vital role in your life. It affects many facets of life as a teen as a young adult. The experiences you have and the lessons you learned during that phase build a foundation for your development as an adult. Often, it determines your response and how you handle tough situations. However, many people fail to realize this.

I always felt inferior to kids who grew up in a home with both parents. I envied them and the life they had. Although I'm grateful for my grandmother, at that time, I couldn't help but wonder how it would've felt if I had both parents to nurture me.

Often, children emulate the things they see or are exposed to, whether positive or negative. For example, if someone experiences a negative childhood, they may develop a negative outlook towards life, or in some cases, their experiences may trigger them to break the negative cycle. The effect of the latter produces a healthy adult life with the determination to be delivered from the things that have trickled down from generation to generation. Therefore, it is important that we serve as good examples to them.

My journey of living with my grandmother started when my mother was diagnosed with Schizophrenia. I am thankful that my grandmother loved us enough to take us (me and my older sister) in because I can only imagine how we would have turned out if she had put us into foster care. My mother was in her early 20's when she was diagnosed, and due to the illness, she could not care for my sisters and me as she should.

However, because she was mentally ill and suffering from paranoia, she was unable to recognize that she was incapable of taking care of us. Hence, she fought my grandmother when she tried to get custody of my younger sister. She felt my grandmother was trying to take her kids from her. As far as she was concerned, she'd rather give my younger sister up for adoption than allow my grandmother to get custody of her.

For a very long time, my mother denied me as her child. Although it may have been a suppressed memory due to her illness, I didn't see it that way. I couldn't bring myself to believe that my mother didn't have any recollection of having me. It was a painful experience for me as a child, and from then, I began to hide my emotions. I didn't want anyone to know how it affected me.

During the course of writing this book, it dawned on me that I actually did not talk about this with many people. I was ashamed to share this with people because there has always been a stigma against mental illness, and I was afraid that they would look at me differently.

For several years, many people have looked at mental illness as a crime. However, this shouldn't be the case. Instead, we must bring awareness to everyone in our society. That way, it would be easier for those suffering from it and their families (African American Community in particular) to come out of their denial to acknowledge the illness and seek immediate medical attention.

I've always known my grandmother to be a strong woman. I can count on one hand the times I've seen her cry or even get emotional. I strongly admired that about her, and gradually, I started becoming like that. I never wanted people to see me cry because I thought it made me look weak. I used to be very hard and had difficulty expressing my emotions. This made me believe that what we experience or witness can formulate our beliefs and emotions.

My grandmother taught us to be independent without needing a man. I think that made me have a negative perception of men. When you have a negative perception about a man, especially from firsthand experience, it can cause you to harbor destructive feelings towards men, whether subconsciously or consciously. For me, I think the negative perception I had towards men developed subconsciously because I didn't realize I had such feelings until I became a teenager. I was always hesitant about getting involved with men in any way. They were all the same and would eventually hurt me as far as I was concerned. Therefore, I built a wall around my heart to prevent myself from getting hurt.

My father was in my life until we had to move from the city. I was only about four years old at that time. My grandmother had received a transfer from the company she worked with, so we had to move to North Carolina because she wanted to raise her family back home in the country with her parents and not in the city. It was then that I lost contact with my father, and since then, we haven't had any contact. I didn't fully understand what was happening as a child, but I couldn't help feeling that my parents had abandoned me. I was so overwhelmed by this feeling that I still struggled with it as an adult. These experiences really took a toll on me because apparently, the two people who were supposed to nurture and love me unconditionally weren't even available and abandoned me. At least that's how I saw it. Hence, I began to doubt everyone who expressed their love for me because I was afraid that they would eventually abandon me like my parents.

The relationship girls have with the first men they encounter, i.e., their father and other men in their immediate family, will shape their perspective towards men in general.

Therefore, it is essential that they are raised in a home where their father is present. A father is usually the best person to show them how they are supposed to be treated as women. Also, for young women to develop a healthy attitude and behavior towards the opposite sex, it is important for them to see interactions between a mother and father or a husband and wife.

Many times, I wished I got to know all of these things earlier. When I became older, I started to realize how hurtful these circumstances were. It caused me so much pain that I was forced to bury it deep down in my heart because I didn't want to admit or acknowledge it. There were some hurtful things that my mother said that I never shared with anyone. Instead, I chose to play the strong role and act as if nothing fazed me when in contrast, it did. They made me afraid for a long time, but now, I actually understand better, and it no longer affects me.

> If you fail to handle hurt and pain properly, it will cause a negative chain of reactions in other areas of your life.

If you fail to handle hurt and pain properly, it will keep building up inside you and cause a negative chain of reaction that may affect other areas of your life. Some of these areas are friendships, relationships, and sometimes parenthood. This reaction keeps working until you become damaged.

Sadly, most people suppress so much hurt and pain from their childhood that it spills into adulthood. They get so accustomed to the numb feeling that they don't even realize they are damaged until something, or someone triggers those feelings. However, if you truly want to heal and get deliverance from these feelings, you must be willing to go through the process.

Many people do not know that one of the effects of having to grow up without one of your parents is the constant feeling of insecurity, which causes all sorts of fears and behavioral complexes. I felt a certain way about myself and everyone around me because the one who was supposed to be the most important male figure in my life had let me down and walked out of my life. Although this may not have been his intention, I just couldn't think of any justifiable reason.

The absence of a father figure affects your self-esteem. Imagine not having someone to reassure you of how much he loves you or tell you how pretty or how special you are at the point that you need to hear it from them. For so long, I searched for answers to my numerous questions about my father. Sometimes, I concluded that it was my fault, but other times, I wanted to get a chance to know why he didn't want to be in my life and why he couldn't do everything in his power to find me.

When answers were not forthcoming, I began to look for love and acceptance in other outlets. Naturally, the outlet may be different for each person. It may be men, women, drugs, alcohol, or some other addiction. My experience with my father made me develop a severe negative outlook towards men. I liked them, but I couldn't bring myself to trust or depend on any man because I saw them as a timing bomb waiting to explode. The moment I let my guard down and let them in, I would get hurt.

I've learned so far that women who were raised in a home with available parents and had positive male figures will most likely know how to interact with a man in a healthy way, while women who were raised in single households tend to learn through their experiences. However, once they reach a certain age, it becomes more difficult to adapt to change and unlearn the toxic knowledge or outlook they have of men and their relationship with them.

Another issue I dealt with as a child was my dark skin color. Society had everyone believing that anyone with light skin was right and pretty, and because of that, I wanted to be light-skinned. I hated my dark skin to the point that I started seeing myself as ugly.

Often, the other kids called me names in reference to my dark skin, which only furthered my ill feelings towards my skin. Some family members would also call me hurtful nicknames. I remember how we would play a game called the dozens growing up, and the first thing they would mention was my dark skin. This act only compounded how I felt about myself.

> Love is a learned behavior and emotion that must be taught and shown by action.

However, I never told them that the name calling hurt me; instead, I suppressed the hurt and forced myself not to show any reaction.

Thankfully, God has healed me in that area. Today, I can confidently say it anywhere that I love my dark skin tone. I am so glad that I epitomize an African American Queen, and I think it is absolutely beautiful. I guess the saying "Time heals all wounds" is a true statement in this case.

Love is a learned behavior, an emotion that must be taught and shown by action. If a person was not raised in an atmosphere where people are affectionate and loving, then it would be almost impossible to adopt that trait. This is because people emulate what they've seen and observed from those closest to them. For example, if a man were raised in a household where his father abused his mother, he would most likely do one of the following; he may see it as the right way and do the same thing when he gets married, or he'd see it as a wrong trait and ensure that he never becomes like his father. Although it takes an extremely strong individual to overcome learned behavior, it is possible.

Even with how things were in my family, I know that I experienced love as a child. Although my family wasn't the most loving where "I love you" was exchanged among us, it was shown in action. It was just expected that everyone looked out for one another.

The most common type of past hurt we experience is normally developed in our family life. Many times, these experiences that we have while growing hits so deep that it hinders proper growth as we get older, and we can't function properly. We endure them for so long that we fail to realize that they are a hindrance to developing healthy relationships. Sometimes it hurts to unleash feelings and emotions that have been suppressed but simply acknowledging them and talking to someone about them helps, especially if it's a non-biased person. Sometimes, some people harbor childhood hurt subconsciously. Therefore, they require extensive searching and therapy to get to the root of bad experiences such as molestation, rape, and other types of abuse that they may have been a victim of.

In conclusion, learned behaviors and habits can be passed down from parents to their kids. Therefore, we need to stop these destructive patterns in their tracks by acknowledging that they exists, and seeking help. If you want to develop a sound and stable adult life, therapy is the best way to identify and deal with the childhood ties that you need to sever. Ultimately, our goal is to help our kids have a healthy childhood and adult lives.

CHAPTER 2

GENERATIONAL TIES

> *"Maintaining love to thousand, and forgiving wickedness, rebellion and sin. Yet he does not leave the guilty unpunished; he punishes the children and their children for the sin of their parents to the third and fourth generation."*- **Exodus 34:7**

Have you ever noticed how there are a lot of alcoholics in some families or that everyone dies at a certain age or from a certain disease or illness? Well, those are common examples of generational curses.

Although many people across the world are unaware of it, some of those who are aware of it do not believe that it is real. However, the truth is, generational curses are very real. The above examples are sufficient proof that they do exist. There are a lot of families that experience these curses that have been passed down from generation to generation. Sadly, most people who never get to know Christ as their savior do not even recognize this and never get deliverance from these ties. But for those that do, God will raise up a person or a group of people to destroy the generational curses in that family.

Generational curses can be traced as far back as our ancient ancestors. However, the good news is that your DNA changes once you accept Christ as your savior. You are no longer under your family's curses, but you are now a child of the Most High God, and your past has been wiped away. This means that the curses have become impotent and would have no effect whatsoever on you. God destroys anything in your genealogy that will try to destroy or kill you. However, you must walk in the authority that He has given us as His children to be free from these strongholds.

I know that there were generational curses in my family. The major one had to do with marriage. Only a few of the women and men were married in my ancestral history. Diabetes was also a generational curse that many people in my family suffered from.

Alcoholism is a major generational curse that many families suffer from. It is common to find someone's grandfather and their father to be alcoholics, and gradually, they also become alcoholics. One may say it was a learned habit, but as much as it may be possible, there is a stronger force attached to it.

I remember one of my past pastors sharing a personal story during a sermon with us. He had always wanted to own a nightclub, but he couldn't figure out why the urge was so strong. After some investigation, he found out that his father had owned nightclubs. Although this may not be a curse per se, it was a generational pattern. Looking back, owning a nightclub probably wouldn't have been the best move because he was already a pastor at that time.

However, if you are sincere about being delivered, God can deliver and set you free from anything that tries to keep you in bondage or afflict your family. This is an assurance that we find in **Psalm 18:2**, He is **Jehovah-Mephalti - Lord my deliverer**.

Some families practice witchcraft and are so deeply rooted in it that they will shun or kill any member of the family who decides not to join the practice. The curse of witchcraft in a family can be destroyed by someone who is a member of the family or one who isn't if they are a born-again believer. However, the person must have the gift of deliverance and the ability to kill demonic spirits. Even though some people do not believe in witchcraft, it is powerfully practiced in many regions of the world. As a matter of fact, there are some places around the world that are specifically known for it.

Breaking free from generational ties is a major hurdle for us all. It is important that we are delivered from all strongholds keeping us away from where God wants us to be. I heard a preacher once say, "Most of us have just developed a strong sense of self-discipline. Just because we don't actually commit the sin doesn't mean we don't want to." In this instance, we haven't been delivered. Therefore, to be delivered means to be set free completely, and there is a process involved.

First, we must identify the areas we need deliverance because *"**The spirit is willing, but the flesh is weak**"* - **Matthew 26:41**. You must also be honest with yourself and God regarding the areas in your life that you need deliverance.

You should always remember that Christianity is a journey, and we are being perfected daily as we walk with God. God is the only one that was perfect and without sin; therefore, He doesn't expect us to be perfect; rather, He expects us to strive to be more like Him every day. In addition, you must remember what **Philippians 1:6** says *"Being confident of this very thing, that He that began a good work in me shall perform it until the day of Jesus Christ."*

I know that God is working on me, and I still haven't completely reached my destiny. It is a gradual and daily journey that I am willing to go through. My prayer is for Him to continue to work through me and also to remove anything that is not of Him.

The true healing for your mind, body, and soul comes when you open up to someone about the deep things in your heart, and through the help of the Holy Spirit, they can discern things that you aren't even aware of. When your spirit is full of God, then it will overflow into the other areas of your life. You and your family will reap the benefits, and your relationships with others will change for the better as well.

However, deliverance is an ongoing process. As long as we are living, we are never truly delivered from everything. There will always be something we need to be delivered from or something that we need God to help us with. There are still several things that I struggle with daily. Therefore, the closer we get to God, the more access we'd have to get delivered from the things that hold us back from being who God has called us to be.

In the bible, God delivered people in very unconventional ways. For example, He once restored the eyesight of a blind man when he spat on the ground, made mud and put it on a man's eyes. He also spoke to people and gave them directions which led to their deliverance. It is safe to say faith played a huge part in the deliverance of those people, as it also plays a part in our deliverance today.

Faith without works is dead, and contrary to popular belief, we must play a part in our deliverance. God won't do all the work not because he can't, but because He expects us to have faith and believe that *all things are possible to those who believe*! It shouldn't be a hard task because we have the same power that rose Jesus from the dead in us. Educating yourself is a crucial component in receiving deliverance.

Understanding what deliverance is will help you identify areas that you may deal with subconsciously or consciously. Learning about your past and your family's past will bring areas of struggle to the forefront and then helps begin the deliverance process.

Another important part of deliverance is counseling. Unfortunately, most people do not have someone that they can completely bare their soul and disclose personal trauma. This is because one must be extremely careful with such delicate information to avoid getting hurt even further.

God didn't intend for us to carry burdens alone and heal ourselves. That is why **James 5:16** says, "*Therefore confess your sins to each other and pray for each other so that you may be healed.*" He wants us as Christians to help one another overcome. But we must be trustworthy when others entrust us with their strongholds.

Although God is the ultimate deliverer, and He is fully capable, He provides several outlets to aid us in our deliverance. However, we must first be open to these outlets. These outlets contain but are not limited to Webinars, books, Seminars, Conferences, etc. Also, there are professional and spiritual counselors out there willing to help you work through your trauma.

I have had the opportunity to have a physical session with a spiritual and professional counselor. I've also had a phone session with both. And to be honest, I recommend it for everyone because I can't even begin to describe the feeling of relief, peace, and freedom that I felt after doing so.

In conclusion, there are so many times our ancestral line holds us back and keeps us in bondage. The enemy uses these curses to destroy families, generations, and legacy. If not dealt with properly, they can have devastating effects that last throughout that family's lineage including death. Demonic spirits such as homosexuality are another example of generational curses. However, it will be discussed further under Demonic Ties in the next chapter.

CHAPTER 3

DEMONIC TIES

"When the unclean spirit goes out of a man, it passes through waterless places seeking rest, and not finding any, it says, 'I will return to my house from which I came'."- **Luke 11:24**

The featured bible text, Luke 11:24-26, gives a detailed account of the deliverance process. The moment a person is delivered from an unclean spirit, the spirit begins to roam through waterless places in search of someone else to possess (a place of rest). If the spirit doesn't find a new place, it will return to the place from which it was previously driven out. However, if it finds the old place swept and in order, it will leave and then return with seven additional spirits more dangerous than itself, making the state of the possessed person worse than it ever was. This means that if you are truly delivered from a thing, it is advised that you shouldn't go back and subject yourself to it or anything related to it. Otherwise, when the unclean spirit infects you again, it will be seven times worse than it was before.

There are several examples of people being possessed with demons in the bible. One notable example is in Matthew 8:28-34. In there, Jesus met two men heavily possessed by a demon whose name was Legion which means 'many.' He spoke to the demons and drove them out of the men. The demons obeyed Jesus and left the men then entered a herd of pigs nearby. The men were delivered from the demonic inhabitation through the gift of deliverance that Jesus possessed. Another notable example is when Jesus healed a mute-demon-possessed man in Matthew 9:32-34. After Jesus drove the demon out, the man regained his speaking ability and began to speak like every normal human being. Asides from these two examples, there are several other accounts of Jesus setting demon-possessed people free with His supernatural healing power.

There are so many different types of demonic spirits that people wrestle with. Unfortunately, many people do not even know about this, and since they don't, it may almost be impossible for them to recognize that they are demon-possessed, not to mention when to seek appropriate help. However, some other people have the power to cast out demons. They are anointed by God and called to operate in the spiritual realm.

For a very long time, I was very skeptical about spiritual things, but after certain experiences I had, I was sure I could boldly refer to myself as a bona fide believer. I remember my first experience of laying hands on someone. I had attended church service earlier that day, and it was so good. The spirit was high that I felt so light and free once I got home. That night while I was in bed, I began to hear the Holy Spirit nudging me to lay hands on a friend that came over to spend the night. I can't remember if I was asleep or awake, but the nudge was so strong that I had to oblige. I went over to where they were and laid hands on them.

As soon as I did that, I saw what looked like fog in the air. Immediately, I started speaking in tongues, and right there, I saw black shadows being released from their body. At that moment, I heard a deep male voice say to me, "Kim, you are making me mad!" But for some reasons I couldn't readily identify the voice, I wasn't scared or intimidated by the unknown masculine voice; instead, I just went on doing my thing. Thinking back, I strongly believe that it was the devil, and I was casting out demons at that moment.

Since many people aren't familiar with demons and demonic spirits, I would highly recommend that they educate themselves on the subject. The bible has many examples of demonic encounters, and as a result, it is a good and foundational tool for knowledge in reference to the subject. In addition, books are also an exceptional tool. A good example is *Frank Hammond*'s book "*Pigs in a Parlor: A Practical Guide to Deliverance*." He also has other books on deliverance and discerning spirits.

Once you are rightly informed, you will find it easy to discern these spirits and start your journey to deliverance. In addition, you will be delivered personally and also become a channel of deliverance to others around you who may also need to be delivered from demonic ties. The purpose of those called into the deliverance ministry is to help others get delivered. God gives them a special gift of being able to either lay hands on people to help them get delivered or to pray for, with and over them.

It is important to note that demonic ties don't only consist of demonic possessions; the enemy can also use people to attack you. He is constantly looking for easily infiltrated people, which he uses to get to the ones he can't reach. This means that when the enemy tries to reach you and fails, he will most likely use the people closest to you. Some vivid biblical examples to support this point are **Job 1:7** - *"The Lord asked Satan 'where have you come from?' Satan answered the Lord, 'From roaming throughout the earth, going back and forth.'"* and **1 Peter 5:8**, which says *"Be sober-minded and alert. Your adversary, the devil, prowls around like a roaring lion, seeking someone to devour."* However, before we try to fight the enemy, we must remember what **Ephesians 6:12** says *"We wrestle not against flesh and blood, but against principalities, against powers, against the rulers of the darkness of this world, against spiritual wickedness in high places."*

Spiritual warfare consists of fighting against the work of preternatural evil forces. Therefore, we need some important tools in our fight against the enemy. Combining constant prayer and fasting is an effective and powerful weapon for spiritual warfare. It has been proven repeatedly as a way of defeating the enemy. Jesus even confirms this in **Mark 9:29** - "*This kind can come out by nothing but prayer and fasting.*" It is important to use these tools because it takes more than the laying of hands for some demons to be cast out. In summary, there is so much to learn when it comes to spiritual things. Therefore, we must "*study to show thyself approved.*" - **2 Timothy 2:15**.

Today, a common practice in most churches is the impartation of spirits. 'Spirits' here refer to the Holy Spirit. The pastors or the preachers may lay hands on the parishioners to fill them with the Holy Spirit. Although until I got hands laid on me, I used to think to myself, "man, that can't be real," whenever I witnessed anything like that.

All I could remember from my experience was that it was a feeling that I'd never felt before. I felt like a weight was being lifted off me at that moment. I was also a little lightheaded as my eyes rolled to the back of my head, and my body felt extremely light as I was falling backward. Sadly, many people are skeptical of this practice which shouldn't be so because the laying of hands dates back to the bible days where Jesus Himself laid hands on people to heal them and also cast out demonic spirits.

Often, we deal with spirits that we aren't aware of until we come across information or meet someone who can discern them. A common yet often unrecognized spirit that many wrestle with is the *spirit of Leviathan*. It is commonly related to the spirit of envy and pride.

Some other demonic spirits are but are not limited to *Python, Behemoth, Marine,* and *Jezebel.* There are so many and too many to name and explain individually. However, once you are exposed to the things of the spirit, you can research and learn to equip yourself with foundational information about these things.

It is important to be aware of things that can attach to your life and possibly destroy you and your legacy. These things would be considered **Strongholds**. Strongholds are things that we deal with spiritually that greatly influence us. No matter how strong the influence is, we need to seek deliverance from them.

Other than the demons or spirits mentioned above, there are some other ones that are sexually related. For example, *Incubus* is a male demon that engages in sexual activity with women while they are asleep, while *Succubus* is the female counterpart that does the same thing but to men. Other demonic spirits include lust, seduction, and infidelity. They are very common demons that many people wrestle with. These are also gateways that develop into Sexual Soul ties.

These demonic spirits can be transferred from one person to another through different means. For example, one can transfer a demonic spirit through sex. It is also how some soul ties and sexual ties are entered into your body. The primary purpose of demonic spirits is to ruin the life of whoever they possess. Once they gain access to a person's body, they begin to control their body and life in general. Demonic spirits can cause poverty, sickness, soul possession, and even death. Having a relationship with Christ and being filled with the Holy Spirit can help ward off a demonic attack. And if you are already demon-possessed, it will help you cut ties with them.

CHAPTER 4

SOUL TIES

> *"What? Know ye not that he which is joined to a harlot is one body? For two, saith he, shall be one flesh."*
> **- 1 Corinthians 6:16**

Soul ties are the intimate bond that one human being shares with another. However, this bond is not limited to a particular set of people. It can be between people of the opposite sex, friends, or a person of authority. A soul tie can either be positive or negative. Therefore, it is necessary that we identify the unhealthy soul ties in our lives and sever them accordingly.

Many of us have soul ties from our past, especially with people that we've had sexual relations with. One may want to argue this since they are no longer connected to them, but the truth is, you create a soul tie with every person you've been intimate with and your soul automatically becomes intertwined with theirs. In my opinion, a sexual tie is one of the most delicate soul ties we deal with as human beings. For example, once a man and a woman get married, they create a soul tie. Even the bible confirms this - "*therefore, the two shall become one.*" Therefore, we must seek to build only positive soul ties.

Relationships are an example of a soul ties. They can help you identify the areas you need to work on in your life. It is obvious that every person in a relationship wants a perfect partner. Well, as much as I hate to rain on your parade, I have to be honest with you. There is no such thing as a "perfect partner." Everyone has faults and hang-ups, which means it is up to you to decide the deal-breakers and the habits you can tolerate.

From research, I know that a common deal-breaker for most people is infidelity. Surprisingly, everyone has the tendency to cheat on their partner. However, it is solely their decision to restrain themselves or to go ahead and give in to it, just like any other addiction or habit. According to compare camp, over 90% of Americans consider infidelity immoral, and around 30% to 40% of Americans cheat on their partners. This data may seem to be one of the reasons we have a higher record of relationships and marriages hitting rock bottom.

That the whole idea of a "perfect partner" is a faux but this doesn't mean you should just settle for anyone who comes your way. The idea is for you to be with someone who brings out the best in you because, in the real sense, that is what is beneficial for both of you

Experiencing a bad relationship is usually very traumatic and emotional but, it may also serve as a learning tool. For example, if you've never had a bad relationship experience, you may never be able to identify the good ones and know how to treat them. We learn so much from past relationships. From personal experience, I can truly say that I've learned a lot from my past relationships, especially the bad ones.

Usually, the problem starts when you let your partner dictate your future.

Following my bad relationship experience, I started to create walls to prevent myself from being hurt again. Whenever I met someone who I thought had the potential to penetrate my heart, I'd put up a wall and become emotionally unavailable just to prevent them from getting in. However, instead of protecting my heart as I expected, it prevented me from experiencing the genuine love and happiness that I deserved.

> The same walls built to keep out hurt, will also keep out love.

Sometimes, we hold on to hurts and failures from past relationships so strongly that they become a piece of heavy baggage, and gradually, this baggage creates a barrier to our happiness and the possibility of future healthy and meaningful relationships. This is because when we experience negative outcomes in relationships, we put up walls that we think are strong enough to prevent us from getting hurt, but unknown to us, it blocks our happiness. It is simple reasoning; if the walls keep out hurt, it's not going to let love in (The same wall built to keep out hurt, will also keep out love).

Soul ties are often formed during dating or courtship. There are different notions about dating. Some people think you should date one person at a time, while others believe you should date multiple people until you find the one you want to be exclusive with and eventually marry. Dating is the process of getting to know someone. However, a lot of people mix this up by dating basically with the intention to marry the person they are dating.

Marriage is sacred and should be treated as such. However, it seems people get married nowadays for the thought of it or, in some way, to hold onto a person. Unfortunately, marriage is never a tool to keep or hold onto a person. If anything, it will drive them away once it's no longer what they want. Many married people still act as if they are single, and this may be linked to the fact that a lot of people see marriage as a business arrangement. However, the bible does not approve of this. Instead, it states that "*And the two shall become one flesh so that they are no longer two, but one flesh.*" - **Mark 10:8**.

Marriage is a union that is honored by God, and if more people saw it the way God does, it would reduce the rate at which marriages end up in separation and divorce. Marriage represents unity, and since the enemy hates any form of unity, he comes after it.

I had the privilege to witness two close marriages. I got to see how they interacted with their husbands and how they served them - cooking and doing most of the household chores. The part that got my attention the most was seeing a wife living a Christian life that caused her husband to come to Christ. This visual representation formed my perspective of marriage as a child. As I grew older, the church helped me to develop an even deeper perspective. I learned what the bible says about marriage and how to be a godly wife.

Love has the power to make you vulnerable. However, most people would rather choose to protect their ego and have some sort of control over their feelings than to be vulnerable. This is because they don't like the fact that love makes them weak to the person they share it with. This feeling of vulnerability makes a lot of men and women skeptical of marriage because they are afraid of falling in love and being fully committed to one person. However, we should note that **2 Timothy 1:7** is a reminder to us - "***God has not*** *given us the spirit of fear, but of power and of love and a sound mind."*

Bad relationships are not restricted to one gender. Both men and women experience it. Unfortunately, this has a huge impact on how we view future relationships. Therefore, you must heal completely from them. Although I understand that this is easier said than done, you must determine in your mind that you are not going to let the past dictate your future. The bible admonishes us in **Isaiah 43:18** - *"Do not remember the former things; neither consider the things of old."* Therefore, you must learn from your past experiences without letting them dictate or hinder the success of your future relationships.

Trust is another big issue in relationships, whether friendship or courtship. There are a lot of cases where people who have been hurt by someone in their past and struggle with trust issues. Often, the hurt they experienced comes from people with whom they've shared ties. For example, parents, siblings, friends, boyfriends, girlfriends, or even the church. Whatever the case, it directly impacts how they perceive people. For example, one of my strongholds is trust issues. After several bad experiences, I started having a hard time trusting people. I had to dedicate myself to praying, fasting, and reading my bible to get through those dark times. I went through therapy, and I still plan on undergoing more therapy in the future. I believe that faith in God and all these methods are sure ways to get deliverance from strongholds.

I know that all of this is a big risk, and you want to protect your heart, but you must know that love itself is a risk. As I grew older, I realized that life is about taking risks. If you don't take risks, you may never hit the jackpot. Yes, you may lose, but if you don't play, you can't win. Entrusting someone with your heart can go either way, but you must focus on the positive side and have faith in God. After all, **Hebrews 11:1** tells us that "*Faith is the substance of things hoped for and the evidence of things not seen.*" When you are in a healthy relationship, and truly in love, you don't mind risking it all for that person.

> Being in Love is one of the most wonderful feelings a human being can experience.

Being in love is one of the most wonderful feelings a human being can experience. In these times, you won't allow fear to hinder you. The bible says in **1 John 4:18**, "*There is no fear in love, but perfect love*

***drives out fear, because fear has to do with
punishment.*** " You'll find yourself smiling more and
being happy generally. Random thoughts about the
person or something they said will bring a smile to your
face or even make you laugh. In addition, forgiveness
is also a big part of the equation. Unforgiveness is like
poison. So, if you are harboring it in your heart, you will
never be able to love someone completely.

Another stumbling block that I've seen destroy
relationships over and over again is what I call the "*Past
Hurt Syndrome.*" From the name, you can already guess
what it is about. It refers to when the hurts and failures
of past relationships cause a person to ruin subsequent
relationships.

Often times, people sabotage themselves, and they
aren't even aware of it. This is simply because Self-
sabotage can come in different ways. One trait of Self-
sabotaging is when a person causes problems where
there aren't any and pushes people away when things
seem to be going well.

For you to move on after a past hurt, you must
totally cleanse yourself mentally and emotionally. It is
advised that people take time to heal and get rid of
baggage from one relationship before entering into

another. However, the time it takes to heal from past hurt differs from one person to the other. I've been through a few bad relationships, but I can say that I learned key lessons from my experiences. Not to mention my experience has greatly contributed to making me the woman I am today.

Another aspect of relationships that we hardly talk about is how people sometimes become victims of other people's past. These relationships are usually toxic because they end up paying for all the hardships and negative experiences their partners had and vice versa.

As earlier discussed, love is a learned behavior. Some people just don't know how to express love because they've never experienced what it feels like to be loved genuinely. Their response to love is developed from their experiences and their past environments.

When I started writing this book, my primary focus was on love and relationships, but after research, I realized that there are so many facets to the relationships in our lives that go way beyond love relationships.

When we get our relationship with God straight, our relationship with humans falls into place. I have come to realize that the closer I get to God, the better my relationships are with people. The reason this happens isn't farfetched - *GOD IS LOVE!* When we give our lives to God and submit to His will and love, we, in turn, learn to love others. This is because the more you love God, the easier it will be for you to love yourself and others.

Research shows there are four main types of love - *Storge*, *Agape*, *Philia*, and *Eros*.

- ♦ **Storge Love**: This is the most natural kind of love. It is mostly exhibited in families or people who have found themselves together by chance. We do not have a choice on this type of love.

- ♦ **Philia Love**: This is the love between friends. Friendship is the strong bond existing between people who share a common interest or activity. We can decide whether or not we want to have this type of love or not. However, a healthy friendship is advisable.

- ♦ **Eros Love**: This is romantic love, the sense of being in love or loving someone.

♦ **Agape Love**: This is unconditional love. It is the greatest kind of love. Agape love is the love God has for us and the kind of love God wants us to have for others. However, the easiest way to access this kind of love is to have a personal relationship with God.

These types of love are further explained in the book *"The Five Love Languages"* by **Gary Chapman**. It helps to determine how you equate love and how to recognize how others equate love as well. I highly recommend everyone read this book.

Moving forward, we must love Christ first then love ourselves before we can begin to love anyone else. God has me in a place where He is settling my mind, thoughts, and soul. He is preparing me for greater levels, and I am learning so much about myself. I am learning to love myself in new ways and learning the things that uniquely make me who I am. I am also learning who I am in Him. I am learning to separate the positive things and people from the negative ones. I am eliminating things and people that are a hindrance to me and my Spiritual growth as well as and other areas. Overall, I am learning how to love and be more loving.

In conclusion, it seems that some of our best and most memorable experiences come when we least expect them. Therefore, if you want to experience love at its greatest capacity, you shouldn't hold back. Instead, let go of all negative soul ties and free your mind, body, and soul to experience the genuine love that you deserve.

CHAPTER 5

TRAUMATIC TIES

Trauma comes in different forms, and it basically hits everyone differently. What one person considers a traumatic situation doesn't mean that someone else would feel the same way. A lot of people experience *Post Traumatic Stress Disorder [PTSD]* due to trauma. PTSD is a mental health condition that is triggered by witnessing or experiencing a terrifying event. I have never been diagnosed with PTSD, but I have experienced some of its symptoms after some traumatic events.

I have had a couple of traumatic events in my life, but I'd say my most traumatic experience was when a close friend raped me. It was an extremely dark phase of my life. I just couldn't bring myself to understand how a person I had trusted so much would betray me like that. The event took a toll on me emotionally, physically, and relationally. I experienced a plethora of emotions. Sometimes I was angry and full of rage; other times, I was afraid as I watched guilt overwhelm me. This traumatic event created problems within my relationships, both romantic and platonic.

Before the incident, I was never as hesitant to trust people. But after it happened, I began to develop trust issues. I didn't believe that people had good intentions towards me. Instead, I began to think that everyone would let me down and hurt me in some way. For a long time, I blamed myself. I couldn't stop thinking about the possibility that things may have turned out differently if I wasn't under the influence of alcohol. I didn't think anyone would believe me, so; I tried extremely hard to completely push the terrifying event out of my memory. I made efforts to act like I was fine, and the whole event never happened.

When someone hurts you, you never really know if you've forgiven them until you see them, and don't feel any negative feelings. I hated my abuser for so long and thought I could never forgive them. Even though I knew that I had to forgive and I really wanted to, I just didn't feel like I'd completely forgiven them. As much as I knew, I was still in the forgiveness process. In June 2019, the unexpected happened. I saw my abuser. I was overwhelmed and extremely shocked when I saw him. Although I didn't speak to him because I saw him from a distance. Though I don't think we would have spoken even if we were in close proximity. Surprisingly, I didn't feel the hatred I had nursed for the longest time; neither did I feel my heart sink into my stomach as I expected. At that moment, I honestly had no ill feelings toward him, and that was my conviction confirmation that I had truly forgiven him. Getting to that point was definitely a long road for me.

My abusive relationship is another traumatic event I went through. I was young, naïve and so full of life. Unfortunately, I ended up in an unhealthy relationship. I was neck-deep in a mental, physical, emotional, and verbally abusive relationship. I was unaware that I was sad and battling depression. Thankfully, I walked away before it was too late.

Sometimes in life, you may have to do yourself the favor of detaching yourself from people that you feel you can't live without. These can be romantic partners, friends, family, and sometimes spiritual leaders. It would be in your best interest if you severed ties with anyone that hinders your overall growth. It may be a challenge, but it is what you need.

Sometimes the noise of the outside world, friends, and family may overshadow your thoughts and make it hard to decipher God's voice and what He is saying to you. In times like that, God may put you in a place of seclusion so He can draw you close to Him and speak to you without distractions.

During these times, you may feel so lonely and as though everyone has abandoned you. But rest assured that that is not the case. God puts you in an incubator to elevate you to the spiritual level he has ordained for you. You should note that discerning God's voice is so important to understand your journey and destiny.

Many times, people will tell you what they think you should or shouldn't do. Although God may use a person to speak to you, the words will only confirm what He has already spoken to you in your spirit. This means that God will never speak something through someone else that he hasn't already shown you or spoken to you about it.

There are many other ways God speaks to His people. However, you must exercise discernment to differentiate between God using someone to speak to you or the enemy using someone to speak to you.

When God speaks to us concerning others, we are normally certain that it's Him, but when it comes to Him speaking to us concerning things in our personal lives, we often question if it is really Him or our desires. I realized that this might be because we are constantly trying to protect ourselves from our traumatic past, so we don't exactly pay much attention to what God says to us. However, the good news is that *God has already created us in His image* - **Genesis 1:27** all we have to do is seek Him. You can do this by asking Him to show you who you really are. Once He reveals your true self and things deep within that are hindering you and not pleasing to Him, you can begin the renewing process. This is when He will change your mind and change your innermost parts to make them more pleasing to Him. **Psalms 51:10-12** is a recommended prayer text. "*Create in me a pure heart, Oh God, and* renew a steadfast spirit within me, do not cast me from your presence or take your Holy Spirit, from me. Restore to me the joy of your salvation and grant me a willing spirit, to sustain me."

CHAPTER 6

TRANSITIONAL TIES

―――――――∞∞∞――――――――

"And we know that in all things God works for the good of those who love him, who have been called according to his purpose."- **Romans 8:28**

S everal things may hinder us from moving to a higher level in life. Sometimes, these hindrances may result from our actions, and other times, it may be beyond our control. Transitional ties are the things that hinder our progress spiritually or naturally.

I gave my life to Christ when I was about 20 years old. I was young and in my first serious relationship. I was living a life of fornication, but I knew that wasn't how I wanted my life to be. All I wanted at that time was to live for Jesus. Unfortunately, it was a battle that I wasn't prepared for because I wasn't even aware of it in the first place. I had to struggle so many times with myself to ensure that I went back on track every time I backslid. After continuous and multiple attempts, I eventually stopped trying. I was overwhelmed by the pressure, and I thought it was too hard to stay on track.

When I had my son at 21, I thought I was grown, and I knew what life entailed. During my first serious relationship, I didn't have any knowledge of how a woman was supposed to interact with her partner or how to treat or react to him. I grew up in a house full of women, so, naturally, I expected to be the center of the relationship. However, I learned that relationships do not always center on the woman; instead, it is a two-way street that involves both parties giving and receiving.

The relationship was an eye-opening experience. I was abused mentally, verbally, emotionally, and even physically. One thing you should know about being a victim of abuse is that your self-esteem, self-confidence, self-worth, and trust will most likely be affected regardless of the form of abuse you experience. Also, abuse can make you nurture hatred towards your abuser and may even hinder your ability to love others. Don't get me wrong, even though my abuser had a couple of flaws, it didn't mean that he was a bad person. For example, he could give someone in need his last just because he felt that the person needed the money more than him. He was just like Dr. Jekyll and Mr. Hide, especially whenever he drank alcohol.

I think he was only a biproduct of his environment and how he was raised.

We learn behaviors, whether good or bad, as a child from the people that are around you. Therefore, it is nearly impossible to have certain traits when you do not have specific examples in your life. I loved my abuser, but he was just never taught how to be a father, a provider, or a man. So, just like me, he was slacking because he didn't know what was expected of him or how he was expected to fit into his role. This is why it's so important to have positive parent figures or role models in your life as a young woman or man; this will aid in your process of growth as an adult.

The relationship took a tremendous toll on me emotionally and physically that I lost so much weight. I weighed less than 100 pounds after giving birth to my son, and even my doctor was concerned about it. I honestly believe that I was experiencing postpartum depression. Adjusting to motherhood and parenting is a significant emotional and physical challenge.

I was raised to always believe in God, but I didn't know the principles of the kingdom and how to live a Godly lifestyle. I knew that there was a God, and he died for my sins, but I didn't know of the power of God and the Holy Spirit. So, for well over nine years, I lived a backslid life. I indulged in all forms of sin. However, God still had a plan for my life despite my sins and confusion. My sins were bad enough, and through my sin trodden life, God still had his hands on me. I knew he still ordered my steps, and all things were working for my good because He chose me. **Psalm 37:23**, which says, "*The Steps of a good man are ordered by the Lord. And He delighteth in his way*", gave me that assurance.

My overall experience in life brought me to my purpose in God. This is not to say that I'm better than anyone. I'm just different. The anointing and calling that God had over my life before the foundations of this world are so great that I can't even fathom it. **1 Corinthians 2:9** reiterates this feeling. It says, "*What no eye has seen, what no ear has heard, and what no human mind has conceived -the things God has prepared for those that love Him.*"

The devil always comes harder for God's chosen. He comes with all guns blazing because he doesn't want God's will for His chosen ones to come into fruition. Therefore, if you are God's chosen, you should be prepared because the devil will come at you in any and every way he can. He plans to steal your anointing because he knows how powerful God's anointing is, and he knows if he can steal that, he can also steal your destiny and purpose in God, which is his ultimate goal. He has been doing this since the beginning of time.

Although no sin is greater than the other, I am forever grateful to God that I never indulged in drugs or prostitution. I rededicated my life to God in 2008. I had recently relocated to Raleigh, NC, and one day, the preacher made the altar call during service, and I felt this strong feeling I'd never felt before. Not long after, I started weeping uncontrollably. There was a continuous tug in my heart, and the urge to go up to the altar was so strong. I already knew a little more about God at that time, but I was still hesitant.

I had been attending church regularly and even bible study, but I still felt there was a void in my life that needed to be filled. I wasn't ready to let go of everything that I knew I wasn't supposed to be doing. So, I thought that if I was going to come to Christ completely, I needed to first get rid of all my sinful behavior and habits.

Unfortunately, this is the most misconceived conception of Christianity. It is a lie that the devil makes us believe to keep us from receiving salvation. If indeed we had the power to overcome without salvation, there would have been no need for Jesus to lay down his life for humanity at the cross. You're not going to be perfect, but you have to keep trying to perfect your walk with God constantly. **Philippians 3:14** reminds us, "*You have to keep pressing toward the mark for the prize of the high calling of God in Christ Jesus.*"

You should note that there will be several road bumps, constructions, and even detours en route to your purpose and destiny. Also, you may have growing pains on your spiritual journey, but you must be persistent as you rely on Paul's word in **2 Timothy 2:3**, "*you have to endure hardness as a good soldier.*"

You must always seek God and ask him to direct your path.

As Christians, hearing from God is so important because it is how we know His plan for our life. But first, you must identify how God speaks to you because he uses different ways to talk to his people. I know that God speaks to me through dreams and visions the same way he did to Joseph in the bible. I'd often sleep and have dreams, only for the dream to come to pass. Also, I've seen countless things in the supernatural and then it would happen in the natural. However, when you are not used to the things of God, it is natural that you'd freak out when these things happen to you. However, the more I learned about God and the supernatural, the easier it was to understand and get comfortable with these gifts.

As humans, there are times that we'd want things to happen at a specific time or in a certain way, but no matter how much we try, it won't happen. This is because we are forcing things to work in our timing instead of God's. However, the moment we rest in God's will, everything will fall into place with ease.

For example, when I was working for the school system, and going to school for my Associate's degree in Tarboro, NC, I tried my best to find a job and move to Raleigh. I submitted multiple job applications, but I got no positive response. Around that time, my house was broken into, and I was afraid to stay there after that. Finally, when I had almost completed my degree, I began to try again, and this time, just as I wanted it, I landed a job in Raleigh. In a matter of one month, I had moved from Tarboro to Raleigh. It was an adjustment that happened so fast that I began to have panic attacks and feel as if my head was spinning.

I didn't understand then why it happened at this time, but God allowed me to stay at my job, which helped me go to school, complete my clinicals, and not worry about losing money. He worked it out, and things fell into place once I was done with school. I needed to move in God's timing but I was trying to move on my timing which was why it wasn't working out. So, this is a classic example of the opening text, **Romans 8:28**, "*And we know that in all things God works for the good of those who love him, who have been called according to his purpose.*"

Although getting robbed was a bad experience, God turned it around for my good. He used it to cause me to move and start another chapter of my life. If that hadn't happened, I'd have probably stayed complacent and stuck.

Even though it is in our human nature to be frustrated, to question God, or even lose faith in the whole process when we don't understand the path that we travel or when things aren't working the way we want them, we must learn to be patient and trust God and His plan. Then, when we look back, we can often connect the dots and put the puzzle together and see that God was actively involved. He is always working things out, even when we don't see the physical evidence. So you must trust that God is working behind the scenes to direct you and lead you in the way you should go.

It may be very challenging and frustrating when God is transitioning you into your purpose. This is because God is working on you spiritually and sifting things out of you to move you to a more excellent place. Therefore, he has to remove feelings, emotions, people, and other things inside of you that may hinder your progress in this new phase and then fill you with more of Him and the things that are imperative to your spiritual growth. These experiences may make you uncomfortable and cause you pain, but you should note that it is only for your good.

In conclusion, life is filled with transitions. While God is working on you, the devil is seeking your downfall. He knows your strongholds, and he will attack you in the area where you are the weakest. So, instead of grumbling and still holding on to the things that God has asked you to let go of, prayerfully rest in His will and prepare to transition into the new phase he has set in motion for you.

CHAPTER 7

DESTINY TIES

"Before I formed you in the womb, I knew you, and before you were born, I consecrated you; I appointed you a prophet to the nations."- **Jeremiah 1:5**

Knowing your purpose in life is very vital. I can say that it is the foundation on which many other essential things in your life are built. When you know your purpose, it'd be easier for you to put the pieces of your life together.

For so long, I was wandering around in life aimlessly, not knowing the purpose God had created for me. But once I accepted Christ in my life as my personal savior, He began to show me my purpose. He started His work in me to create what He predestined before the foundations of the world.

I began to see that certain things were happening in my life that I wasn't paying attention to. Aside from dreams and visions, God spoke to me through prophetic songs. Often, the songs pertained to someone or something in my life. I realized that God called me to be a prophetic singer and that He gave me songs in my spirit and even in my dreams. Although I am passionate about songs and love to sing, I can boldly say the songs that I hear aren't just because I am passionate about singing but because God has a message for me in response to my prayers.

You must find the thing that takes you into His presence. One of the most significant ways I experience His presence is through song. I usher in His presence when I am worshipping and praising Him. I love to do this because it is a way to show Him how grateful I am for all He has done in my life. God inhabits the praise of His people because He loves it when they worship

Him in spirit and truth. So, when we praise God, He is right there with us, dwelling in us.

We may feel that God is not with us when we go through hard times. But instead of feeling discouraged, all we have to do is remember the times He came through for us in the past and made a way where we least expected. I have experienced it countless times. For example, I've been in many situations where I needed to pay my bills, but I didn't know how to do it, but I trusted God, and he came through for me.

I remember the first time God spoke to me. I was looking for an apartment that day, and I wasn't making any headway. After several searching attempts, I was beginning to get frustrated and discouraged. Then, as I was driving, I heard a small still voice say, "go down that road." Before that day, I had never driven on that road, so I began to wonder why I should make the turn. Despite my apprehension, I took the turn down the road and saw a **For Rent** sign on a property. Immediately, I called the number and left a message on the voicemail.

When I spoke to the landlord, I explained that my credit was not the best. This was when I was younger and didn't make the best choices financially. He still accepted my application. However, he called me a few days later to inform me that he couldn't take the risk because of my credit. After assuring him that I understood, I ended the call. After the call, I was a little sad and disappointed. I began to think, and then I said to myself, "I refuse to take no for an answer." I began to think God wouldn't have told me to call if this wasn't the apartment for me.

I called him back to request a chance to prove that I was trustworthy. I went as far as to offer him a double deposit, which I think did the trick. Finally, he agreed to meet with me in person to confirm my sincerity, so we scheduled an appointment for the next week. We met as arranged, and needless to say, I was approved, and I moved in. I spent four years in that house until I moved to Raleigh in 2008.

That experience is a perfect example of how God doesn't need our permission to direct our paths. So Naturally, I would never have thought to turn on that road, but God's thoughts are higher than ours. Ever since then, I always pray for God's direction and leading in my life.

One of the issues that many of us face is how to determine our purpose. What you need to know first is that your purpose is the reason for which you were born. It is what God predestined for you to do before the foundations of the world. I've learned if you regularly give yourself to prayer and fasting, it will be easier for you to identify your purpose. Most people believe their passion is their purpose. While this may be accurate in some cases, in my opinion that thing you do well without knowing or hesitating is your purpose.

> Once you understand how God speaks to you, it will help you understand your life and season.

For some reason, most of the people in my circle confide in me. They talk to me about their problems, relationship, spirituality, and everything else. They say I'm a good listener, and they find it easy to talk to me. As much as this may sound like mere compliments, I have come to realize that it isn't. One of my life's purposes is to minister to people. So, while the rest of the world sees it as a trait, I know it is goes far beyond that. I am called to be a minister and an evangelist. In addition, I know that I am called to help people with their relationships and marriage. The area the enemy fights us the hardest is usually the area we are called to minister in. I've gained so much knowledge and experience from all the things

I've gone through in life. These things are now considered a testimony for me to minister to others and help them.

Once you realize how God speaks to you, it will help you understand your life and season. However, you must not be ignorant of the vices of the devil.

He will start playing on your weakness when he sees that you are about to enter into that long-awaited season. For me, I know that he brings fear whenever a big blessing is on the way for me. But God always gives me the strength to trust and rely on Him completely to bring His plan to completion.

Courage is not having the strength to go on; it is going on when you don't have the strength. Sometimes the journey of life is far beyond our understanding. At some point, we may not understand why some events take place, but we will in due time. It is also important to make sure you have the right people in your circle.

Pray and ask God to reveal those who care for you and those who don't. Ask Him to remove you from unhealthy relationships, and He will do just that. You must discern the people that were placed in your life to help you fulfil your destiny and purpose. Remember that having a few godly people is better than many frenemies.

One of the main forms of deliverance is deliverance from people. So often, people unknowingly walk into bondage because they try to gain acceptance from other people. However, you should know that those who genuinely care about you will accept you for who you are and not try to make you who they want you to be.

This does not mean that your friends cannot point out your negative behaviors; it just means that the relationship is unhealthy if they force you to be who you know you aren't. You need to be what God wants and calls you to be. This was an area that I struggled with dearly. I cared more about others' feelings than my own. I wanted to make everyone happy regardless of how unhappy I was, and I ended up paying dearly.

Sometimes people and their moods and spirit can alter our moods and spirit. However, we have a choice to either allow it or block it. One of the best ways to counter the enemy is praise and worship. You can also speak the word. For example, you can say, "the devil is defeated, but God is exalted!" When you proclaim words like this, you are reassured that God is always there to fight your battles. First, however, you must operate in faith.

In addition, you must be careful with who you tell your dreams and visions to. Some people are dream killers. Not everyone that you think loves and care about you is genuine. Some people get close to you just to know what you are doing so they can try to deter your progress. Unfortunately, these people can be family and close friends.

The story of Joseph in the bible is a vivid example of this. God gave him prophetic dreams, but he unknowingly revealed them to the wrong people (his brothers). They were so envious that they tried to kill him. Joseph endured years of trials and tribulations, but God turned it around for his good; what the enemy meant for evil. Therefore, we must trust Him to direct our paths strategically.

We must never forget that the bible was written for our knowledge and to give us instructions for life. No matter what the enemy throws our way, God is All-knowing, and He will always bring us out. So, if you're going through a difficult phase now, just know that the devil is busy trying to block your destiny, but *if God be for you, who can be against you?*

Our faith may be tested several times so that we may trust His faithfulness because He is arranging things in our favor and making a way even when we don't see it or feel it. There are times when God wants us to move or act, and there are also times when He wants us to be still and know that He is God. It is up to you to differentiate and act accordingly.

In conclusion, I've come to realize that everything we go through is not only for or about us. They will help us to birth our purpose in life. Our experiences help us guide others through things we've been through, so they won't have to go through them, and if they do, they'll know how to overcome them.

CONCLUSION

I was just sitting in the room one day when I had an epiphany. I had a revelation from God to write a book and share my personal experiences to help others get delivered. So I got up, went to the computer, and then started writing the book, and almost immediately, the title came to me. Writing this book has been a form of healing and deliverance for me because, for the first time, I am sharing things that I've never told anyone.

Deliverance is a continual process and an everyday journey.

You can Sever the Ties by first acknowledging who or what you need to remove from your life and what's keeping you in bondage. Once you overcome that hurdle, the real work begins, and that could consist of therapy and spiritual guidance.

As humans living on the earth, we are flawed and will forever be seeking total deliverance. I don't speak as someone who has overcome everything I've dealt with, but I am only sharing experiences that have changed me and caused me to analyze things that can help others.

Thinking back over my life, I'm so grateful that I could learn these things before it is too late. I am still learning, growing, and overcoming every day. I also hope that one will read this and want to learn more. I am not an expert on spiritual things; but I've just learned some things in my 40 plus years of living. Hopefully, by reading my experiences and insight, someone will seek more knowledge and deliverance in their life.

CPSIA information can be obtained
at www.ICGtesting.com
Printed in the USA
BVHW070308310123
657438BV00001B/154